b small publishing

# ITALIAN FUN

**Ciao, sono italiana.
Mi chiamo Maria.**

chow sono italee-ana
mee keeah-mo mareea

*Hello, I'm Italian.
My name is Maria.*

**Hello, I'm American.
My name is Peter.**

*Ciao, sono americano.
Mi chiamo Peter.*

chow sono ameree-cano
mee keeah-mo Peter

Catherine Bruzzone
and Lone Morton
Illustrations by Louise Comfort

**ciao!**
chow
*hello, hi*

**buongiorno**
bwon-*jorno*
*good morning*

**buona sera**
*bwona saira*
*good evening*

**buona notte**
*bwona not*-teh
*good night*

**arrivederci**
aree-ved-*air*-chee
*good-bye*

# Ciao!...

Cut out the Italian words below. Put them in the speech bubbles and practice the different greetings. Read them aloud.

**ciao**

**ciao**

**buongiorno**

**buongiorno**

**buona sera**

**buona sera**

**buona notte**

**buona notte**

**arrivederci**

**arrivederci**

Keep the words and you can play the game again.

First write in your name and age. Then fill in the correct ages in Italian below and read them aloud.

Mi chiamo ........................................

Ho ............ anni.

12

8

Ho ............ anni.

Ho ............ anni.

2

5

Ho ............ anni.

7

Ho ............ anni.

Ho ............ anni.

**Mi chiamo...**
mi kee*ah*-mo
*My name is...*

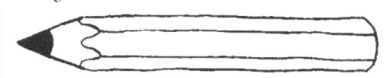

**Ho ... anni.**
o ... *an*-nee
*I am ... years old.*

1 **uno** *oo*no
2 **due** *doo*-eh
3 **tre** treh
4 **quattro** *kw*atro
5 **cinque** *ching*kweh
6 **sei** s*ay*ee
7 **sette** *set*-teh
8 **otto** *ot*-to
9 **nove** *n*oveh
10 **dieci** dee*eh*-chee
11 **undici** *oon*-deechee
12 **dodici** *doh*-deechee
13 **tredici** *treh*-deechee
14 **quattordici**
   kwah-*tor*-deechee
15 **quindici**
   *kwin*-deechee
16 **sedici**
   *say*-deechee
17 **diciassette**
   deecha-*set*-teh
18 **diciotto**
   dee*chot*-toh
19 **diciannove**
   deecha-*n*oveh
20 **venti** *ven*-tee

*You'll find the numbers up to 100 on the inside cover.*

3

## Dov'è...?

dov-*eh*
*Where is...?*

## Dove sono...?

d*oveh* sono
*Where are...?*

Read these questions aloud in Italian. Check off the list when you have found each item.

## Dov'è Roma?
d*oveh* roma
*Where is Rome?*

## Dov'è l'aereo?
d*oveh* la-*aire*ho
*Where is the plane?*

## Dove sono i limoni?
d*oveh* sono ee lee-*monee*
*Where are the lemons?*

## Dove sono le Alpi?
d*oveh* sono leh alpee
*Where are the Alps?*

## Dov'è la nave?
d*oveh* lah *nah*-veh
*Where is the ship?*

## Dove sono le mucche?
d*oveh* sono leh *mook*-keh
*Where are the cows?*

## Dove sono i pesci?
d*oveh* sono ee *peshee*
*Where are the fish?*

4

# Dov'è...?

Italy is in Europe. It is bordered by four other European countries and two seas. Some of the names have been left off this map. Can you fill in the missing names, in English?
*Answers and Italian pronunciation on the inside cover.*

2 La Svizzera

3 L'Austria

4 La Slovenia

1 La Francia

6 L'Adriatico

Roma

Italy
L'Italia

5 Il Mediterraneo

Do you know the colors of the Italian flag? Find out and color in this flag.

# Dov'è…?

Mark and Susan are lost. Can you help them find their way to the station? (*Answer on the inside cover.*)
Read the questions in the margin aloud in Italian.
Find each place on the map and check it off the list.

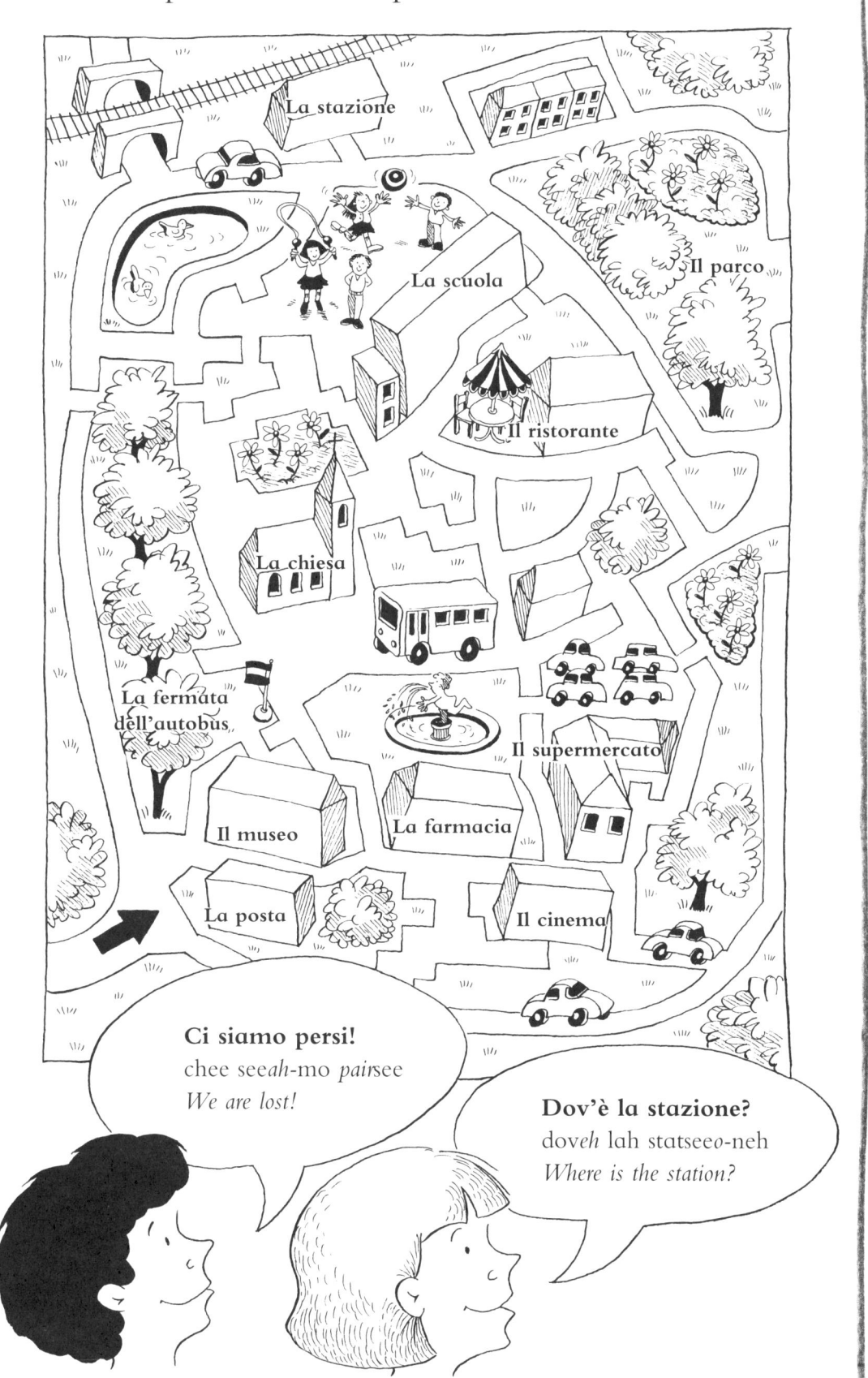

*Map labels:* La stazione, La scuola, Il parco, Il ristorante, La chiesa, La fermata dell'autobus, Il supermercato, Il museo, La farmacia, La posta, Il cinema

**Ci siamo persi!**
chee seeah-mo pairsee
*We are lost!*

**Dov'è la stazione?**
doveh lah statseeo-neh
*Where is the station?*

**Dov'è il parco?**
doveh eel parko
*Where is the park?*

**Dov'è la scuola?**
doveh lah skwoh-la
*Where is the school?*

**Dov'è la posta?**
doveh lah posta
*Where is the post office?*

**Dov'è il cinema?**
doveh eel cheen-ehma
*Where is the movie theater?*

**Dov'è il ristorante?**
doveh eel ristoran-teh
*Where is the restaurant?*

**Dov'è il museo?**
doveh eel moozeh-o
*Where is the museum?*

**Dov'è la fermata dell'autobus?**
doveh lah fairmata del-aow-toboos
*Where is the bus stop?*

**Dov'è il supermercato?**
doveh eel supermair-cah-to
*Where is the supermarket?*

**Dov'è la chiesa?**
doveh lah keeeh-za
*Where is the church?*

**Dov'è la farmacia?**
doveh lah farmasee-a
*Where is the pharmacy?*

**…per favore**
pair favoreh    *… please*

**Che cosa è?**

keh cosa eh

*What is it?*

**Che cosa sono?**

keh cosa sono

*What are they?*

**È…**

eh

*It's…*

**Sono…**

sono

*They are…*

**È una gomma.**

eh oona gom-ma

*It's an eraser.*

**Sono matite.**

sono matee-teh

*They are pencils.*

**È un tavolo.**

eh oon tahvolo

*It's a table.*

**È un righello.**

eh oon reeg-el-lo

*It's a ruler.*

**È uno zaino.**

eh oono tsahee-no

*It's a backpack.*

**Sono libri.**

sono leebree

*They are books.*

**Sono forbici.**

sono for-beechee

*They are scissors.*

**È una sedia.**

eh oona say-deea

*It's a chair.*

# Che cosa è?

Join the dots to find out! Count in Italian as you go. Then write the answers in Italian underneath.

*The numbers from 21 to 100 and the answers are on the inside cover.*

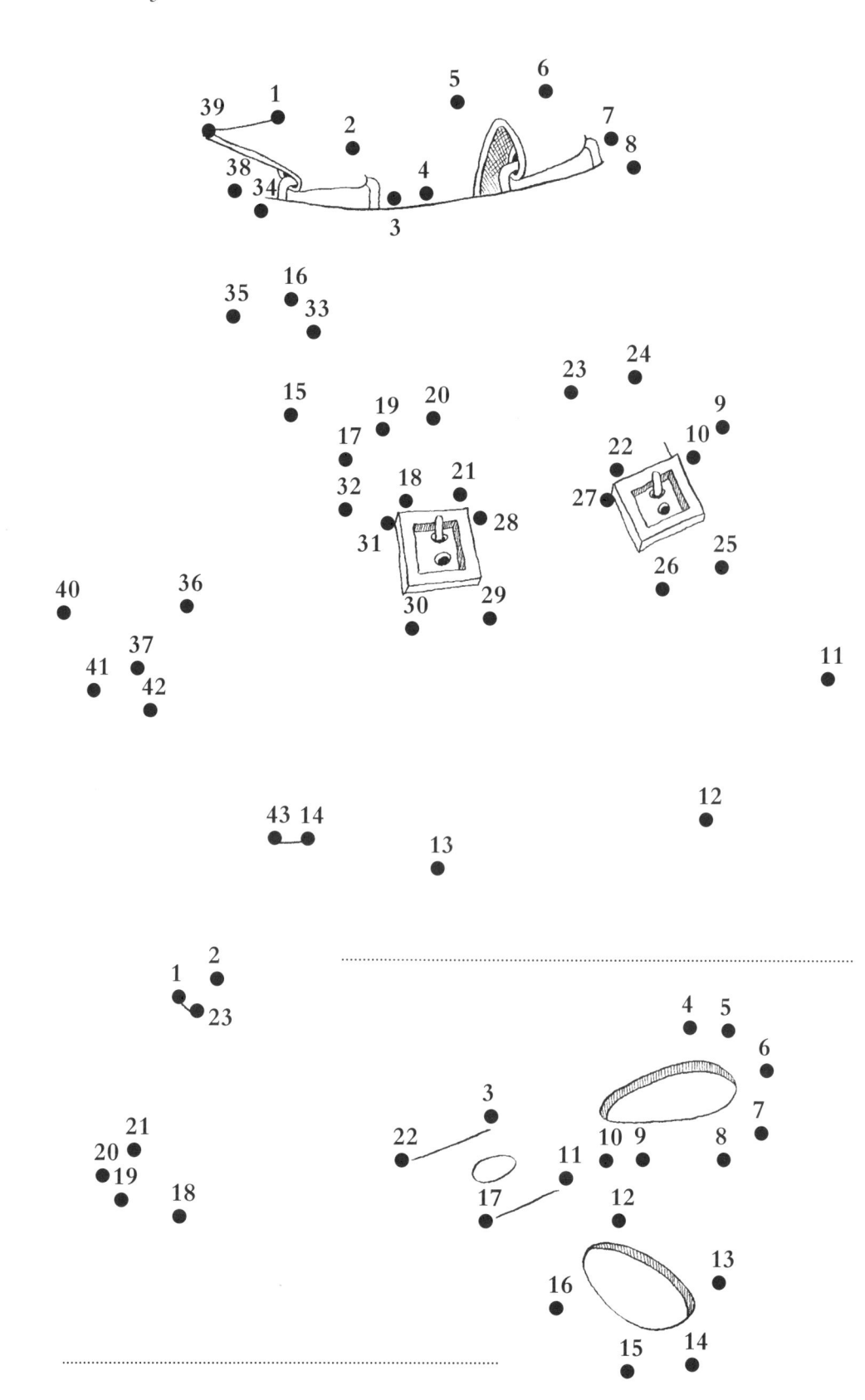

# Match these up!

Match up these pictures, then practice saying the words aloud in Italian. You'll need two dice. Throw one die or two dice, as you like, and say the Italian name for the picture that corresponds to the number you threw.

**il pettine**
eel *pet*-teeneh
*comb*

**il gatto**
eel *gat*-to
*cat*

**il portauovo**
eel porta-*wo*-vo
*egg cup*

**le scarpe da calcio**
leh *skar*peh dah *cal*-cho
*soccer shoes*

**i gattini**
ee gat-*tee*nee
*kittens*

**la teiera**
lah tay-*aira*
*teapot*

**il secchiello**
eel sek-kee-*el*-lo
*pail*

**il pallone da calcio**
eel pal-*lo*-neh dah *cal*-cho
*soccer ball*

**l'uovo**
loo-*wo*-vo
*egg*

**la tazza**
lah *tats*-a
*cup*

**la pala**
lah *pah*-la
*shovel*

**la spazzola per capelli**
lah *spats*-ola pair cap*el*-lee
*hairbrush*

**Mi piace.../
Mi piacciono...**
mee pee-*a*-cheh/
mee pee-*a*-chono
*I like...*

**Non mi piace.../
Non mi piacciono**
non mee pee-*a*-cheh/
non mee pee-*a*-chono
*I don't like...*

**il sole**
eel *so*-leh
*sun*

**i pesci**
ee *pay*-shee
*fish*

**il castello di sabbia**
eel cas*tel*-lo dee *sab*-bya
*sandcastle*

**le onde**
leh *on*deh
*waves*

**le alghe**
leh *al*-gay
*seaweed*

**l'ombrellone**
lombrayl-*lon*eh
*beach umbrella*

**il salvagente**
eel salva-*jen*teh
*float ring*

**il granchio**
eel *gran*-keeyo
*crab*

**i gabbiani**
ee gab-bee-*yah*-nee
*seagulls*

**la palla**
lah *pal*-la
*ball*

8

# Mi piace...

Look at this beach scene and circle ten things you like. Then say them out loud in Italian. Start with '**mi piace...**' (singular) or '**mi piacciono...**' (plural).

**il golf**
eel golf
*sweater*

**il cappello**
eel cap-*pel*-lo
*hat*

**il vestito**
eel ves*tee*to
*dress*

**i pantaloni**
ee pantal*oh*-nee
*pants*

**il costume**
eel cos*too*meh
*swimsuit*

**le calze**
leh *cal*-tseh
*socks*

**le scarpe**
leh *skar*-peh
*shoes*

Cut carefully around these clothes to dress the characters.

**la maglietta**
lah mal-*yet*-ta
*T-shirt*

**la sciarpa**
lah *shar*pa
*scarf*

**il cappotto**
eel cap-*pot*-to
*coat*

**i guanti**
ee *guan*tee
*gloves*

**i pantaloncini**
ee pantalon-*cheenee*
*shorts*

**la gonna**
lah *gon*-na
*skirt*

**il pigiama**
eel pee-*ja*ma
*pajamas*

**gli stivali**
l-yee steev*a*-lee
*boots*

**il berretto**
eel bair*et*-to
*cap*

# Non mi piace...

Now circle four things you don't like.
Say them out loud in Italian. Start with '**non mi piace**' (singular) or '**non mi piacciono**' (plural).

### Quanti pesci?
*kwantee pay-shee*
How many fish?

How many fish can you find in the picture?
*Answer on the inside back cover.*

**il cappello**
eel cap-*pel*-lo
*sun hat*

**la conchiglia**
lah kon*keel*-ya
*shell*

**la spiaggia**
lah spee*ah*-ja
*beach*

**l'asciugamano**
lashooga-*mah*-no
*towel*

**la barca a vela**
lah *b*arka ah *vay*-la
*sailboat*

**il picnic**
eel peek-*neek*
*picnic*

**lo squalo**
lo *skwah*-lo
*shark*

**il costume**
il cost*oo*-meh
*swimsuit*

**la radio**
lah *r*adeeo
*radio*

**gli occhiali da sole**
l-yee ok-kee-*yah*-lee da *s*oleh
*sunglasses*

**la medusa**
lah me*d*ooza
*jellyfish*

### Quanti?
*kwantee*
How many?

9

**la famiglia**
lah fa*meel*-ya
*family*

**la madre/mamma**
lah *ma*-dreh/*mam*-ma
*mother/mom*

**il padre/papà**
eel *pah*-dreh/*pap-a*
*father/dad*

**la sorella**
lah sor*el*-la
*sister*

**il fratello**
eel frat*el*-lo
*brother*

**la nonna**
lah *non*-na
*grandmother*

**il nonno**
eel *non*-no
*grandfather*

**il bebè**
eel beh-*beh*
*baby*

**i genitori**
ee jenny-*toree*
*parents*

**la figlia**
lah *feel*-ya
*daughter*

**il figlio**
eel *feel*-yo
*son*

**i gemelli**
ee je*mel*-lee
*twins*

# La famiglia

Match up the family members. Now label them in Italian. You may find there is more than one way to describe each person. *Answers on the inside cover.*

# Il bar

Practice ordering snacks in a coffee shop.
Play this game with a partner. Pretend you are ordering at this café. Use the picture to help you.
The first player orders, say, '**un caffè, per favore**.'
The next player repeats the order but adds something else, say, '**un caffè e un gelato, per favore**.'
The winner is the last person to say the whole list correctly in the right order.

**il bar**
eel bar
*coffee shop or café*

**un gelato**
oon jel*ah*-to
*ice cream*

**una fetta di dolce**
oona *fet*-ta dee *dol*-cheh
*a piece of cake*

**un cappuccino**
oon cap-poo-*chee*no
*coffee with milk*

**un tè**
oon teh
*a tea*

**un panino…**
oon pan*ee*-no
*a … sandwich*

**…al prosciutto**
al pro*shoot*-to
*…ham*

**…al formaggio**
al for*mah*-jo
*…cheese*

**un succo d'arancia**
oon *sook*-ko da*ran*-cha
*an orange juice*

**una cioccolata calda**
oona choc-*cola*-ta *calda*
*a hot chocolate*

**un bicchiere d'acqua**
oon bik-*kyaireh dak*wa
*a glass of water*

**Quanto costa?**
*kwanto costa?*
*How much is it?*

**Vorrei**
vor-*ray*
*I'd like…*

**il mercato**
eel mair*cah*-to
*market*

**dei pomodori**
dayee pom-oh-*doree*
*some tomatoes*

**delle pere**
*del*-leh paireh
*some pears*

**delle banane**
*del*-leh ban*ah*-neh
*some bananas*

**delle fragole**
*del*-le *frah*-go-leh
*some strawberries*

**delle carote**
*del*-le c*aroh*-teh
*some carrots*

**delle mele**
*del*-le *may*-leh
*some apples*

**delle patate**
*del*-le pat*ah*-teh
*some potatoes*

**una lattuga**
oona lat-*too*-ga
*a lettuce*

**un cetriolo**
oon chetree-*oh*-lo
*a cucumber*

**delle cipolle**
*del*-le cheep*ol*-leh
*some onions*

# Vorrei…

You are going shopping. Read the two shopping lists aloud. Start with '**vorrei….**' Then cut out the items you need below and fill the correct basket.

Il mercato

pere
un cetriolo
pomodori
cipolle
carote
patate
mele
fragole

# Il supermercato

Can you find the coin purse hidden in each picture?

*Shopping list:*
- burro
- marmellata
- pane
- yogurt
- sciampo
- zucchero
- patatine
- biscotti

**il supermercato**
eel supermair-*cah*-to
*supermarket*

**del sapone**
del sapo*neh*
*some soap*

**dello sciampo**
del-lo *sham*-po
*some shampoo*

**dei biscotti**
dayee bis*cot*-tee
*some cookies*

**dello yogurt**
del-lo *yo*goor
*some yogurt*

**delle bevande**
*del*-leh bev*and*-eh
*some drinks*

**dello zucchero**
del-lo *tsook*-kairo
*some sugar*

**della marmellata**
*del*-la marmel-*lah*-ta
*some jam*

**del burro**
del *boo*-ro
*some butter*

**del pane**
del *pah*-neh
*some bread*

**delle patatine fritte**
*del*-leh pata*tee*-neh *freet*-teh
*some potato chips*

**un borsellino**
oon borsel-*leen*o
*a coin purse*

13

## Across

1. You use this to carry things on your back.
3. You can boil or scramble this.
5. Shoes for soccer.
7. Somewhere you would go for a picnic.
8. It makes your skin tanned.
9. A place where you go to see old things.
10. You drink this from a teapot.
11. This swims in the sea.

## Down

1. It is very sweet.
2. Your mother's mother.
4. This protects you from the sun.
6. You buy stamps here.
7. A kind of fruit.
8. cinque, ---, sette.

## Wordsearch

Find the Italian for these words, then circle them on the wordsearch. (They are all words you have already seen.)

FATHER
SHOVEL
APPLES
CAT
CHOCOLATE
BROTHER
BREAD
WAVES
JAM
CUCUMBER

# Crossword & wordsearch

Using the words you can have learned in Italian, fill in this crossword. Then do the wordsearch below. *Answers on the inside cover.*

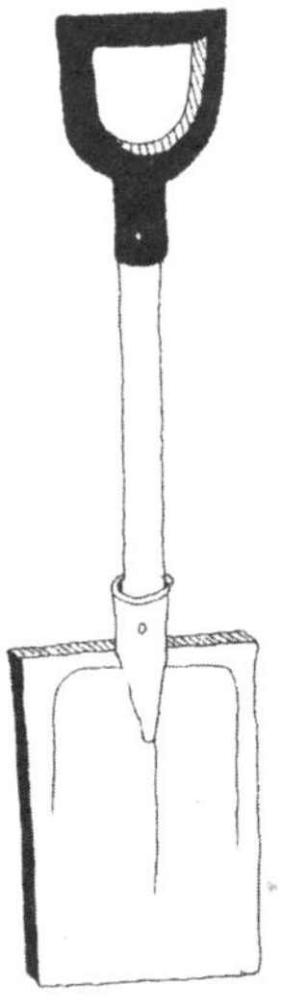

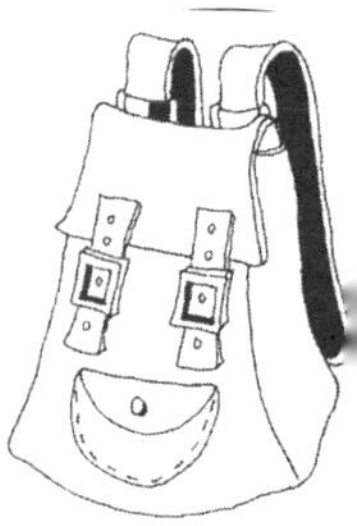

```
P A D R E Q A C O L
A M E L E N E I N G
L M A Z O F S O T A
A S O F P R U C L T
N O R E P A M C S T
D O N O A T I O U O
M R T D N E G L V A
M A R M E L L A T A
S B P R D L F T H I
C E T R I O L O N C
```

14

# Spot the difference

There are eight differences between these pictures. Can you find them?
How many things can you name in Italian? The new words are given.

**la tenda**
lah *tenda*

**l'aquilone**
lakwee-*lo*neh

**la mucca**
lah *moo*-kah

**gli stivali**
l-yee stee*va*-lee

**il giubbotto di salvataggio**
eel joob-*bot*-to dee salva*tah*-jo

**l'anatra**
*lanatra*

**gli anatroccoli**
l-yee ana*trok*-kolee

**la pagaia**
lah pa*gah*-ya

**la canoa**
lah *kanowa*

15

# Italian fortune teller!

First color in the four corners. Then cut out the square along the solid line. Fold back the corners along the diagonal dotted lines. Turn over (so you can read the colors and numbers) and fold back the corners again along the diagonals. Fold in half (backwards) both ways.
Now play!

## How to play
1. Insert the finger and thumb of each hand into the four pockets.
2. With the four corners tightly together, ask a friend to choose one of the four colors.
3. Spell out the color in Italian, opening and closing the *fortune teller* each time. Use the pronunciation guide for the letters of the alphabet. *(The full A-Z is on the inside cover.)*
4. On the final letter, ask your friend to select a number from inside.
5. Then count out the number in Italian, opening and closing as before.
6. Ask your friend to choose another number, and count it out in Italian again.
7. Your friend selects a final number and you read the message underneath!

**blu** — bloo — *blue*
**verde** — vairday — *green*
**giallo** — jal-lo — *yellow*
**rosso** — rosso — *red*

5 cinque
3 tre
7 sette
6 sei
4 quattro
2 due
1 uno
8 otto

**Vincerai la lotteria.** veenchair-ahee lah loterea — *You'll win the lottery.*
**Sei divertente.** sayee deevair-tenteh — *You're fun.*
**Sei un maiale!** sayee oon my-ahleh — *You are a pig!*
**Hai fortuna.** ahyee fortoona — *You're lucky.*
**Baciami!** bacha-mee — *Kiss me!*
**Diventerai celebre.** deeventeh-rahee chaldaybreh — *You'll be very famous.*
**Mi fai ridere.** mee fahee reedereh — *You make me laugh.*
**Ti amo!** tee ah-mo — *I love you!*